Fresh & Fun
Summer

BY PAMELA CHANKO

SCHOLASTIC
PROFESSIONAL BOOKS

NEW YORK • TORONTO • LONDON • AUCKLAND • SYDNEY
MEXICO CITY • NEW DELHI • HONG KONG

For Dexter, who taught me everything there is to know about having—and being—a best friend.

Many thanks to Terry Cooper for walking by my desk at an opportune moment and noticing me; to Deborah Schecter for her willingness to explore the idea; and to Joan Novelli for her unfailing patience, hard work, sense of humor, and great ear for poetry. I would also like to thank each teacher who contributed his or her ideas to this book: Mary Jane Banta, Mitzi Fehl, Rita Galloway, Bob Krech, Deborah Rovin-Murphy, Catherine Wenglowski, and Bobbie Williams. They are all out there every day, changing the world one child at a time.

"Make New Friends" from THE DITTY BAG by Janet E. Tobitt. Reprinted by permission of GSOSA.

"two friends" from SPIN A SOFT BLACK SONG by Nikki Giovanni. Copyright © 1971, 1985 by Nikki Giovanni. Reprinted by permission of Farrar, Straus & Giroux, LLC.

Poster illustration(s) copyright © 2000 by Giovanni Manna, from SOMEONE I LIKE, originally published by Barefoot Books, Inc.

Scholastic grants teachers permission to photocopy the reproducible pages from this book for classroom use. No other part of this publication may be reproduced in whole or in part, or stored in a retrieval system, or transmitted in any form or by any means, electronic, mechanical, photocopying, recording, or otherwise, without permission of the publisher. For information regarding permission, write to Scholastic Professional Books, 555 Broadway, New York, NY 10012-3999.

Produced by Joan Novelli
Front cover, interior, and poster design by Kathy Massaro
Cover and interior art by Shelley Dieterichs
Poster art by Giovanni Manna

ISBN 0-439-21610-9
Copyright © 2000 Scholastic Inc.
Printed in the U.S.A.
All rights reserved.

Contents

About This Book 4
Summer Activity Calendar 5

Bugs

Bug Bingo 6
BOOK BREAK: *When the Fly Flew In...* 6
Insect or Not? 6
BOOK BREAK: *The Very Hungry Caterpillar* ... 7
A Caterpillar's Calendar 7
Caterpillar's School-Day Snack 7
"The Riddle of the Bugs" Mini-Play 8
Closeup on Bugs 8
The Buggy Song 9
BOOK BREAK: *Audubon First Field Guides: Insects* 9
Collaborative Bug Banner 10
BOOK BREAK: *A Bug Research Library* 10
Ladybug Math Story Mat 11
One Honey of a Treat! 11
Reproducible Activity Pages 12–16

Patriotism

Independence Day Parade 17
Secret Ballot Box 17
BOOK BREAK: *Betsy Ross* 18
Measure the Statue of Liberty 18
Design a Class Flag 19
BOOK BREAK: *The Flag We Love* 19
Singing and Signing the Red, White, and Blue .. 19
Reproducible Activity Page 20

Old Friends, New Friends

Teaching With the Poster: "two friends" 21
BOOK BREAK: *Best Friends for Frances* 22
Twenty-First Century Pen Pals 22
BOOK BREAK: *Best Friends* 22
Friendship Pocket Calendar 23
Secret Pal Messages 23
Old Friends and New Friends Mini-Book ... 24
Facts About Friends 24
Silver and Gold Friendship Circles 25
Old Friends...Young Friends! 25
BOOK BREAK: *Wilfrid Gordon
   McDonald Partridge* 25
BOOK BREAK: *Free to Be...You and Me* 26
Friendship Hearts 26
Reproducible Activity Page 27

Summer Fun

Beach Ball Math 28
Hide-and-Seek With Shells 28
BOOK BREAK: *Greetings From Sandy Beach* .. 29
Sun Shadow Clock 29
BOOK BREAK: *Sun Song* 29
Sun Prints 30
BOOK BREAK: *The Way to Start a Day* 30
Sun Safety Puppets 31
Where Do Puddles Go? 31
Reproducible Activity Page 32

"two friends" poetry poster .... *bound in center*

About This Book

When most people hear the word *summer*, they think of sandy beaches, swimsuits and sunglasses, vacations, barbecues, and so on. And summer does, in fact, include many of these pleasures. However, the one thing people (especially small ones) usually do *not* associate with summer is the word *school*. Well, if you picked up this book, it means you are teaching children this summer. And whether you are teaching at a year-round school, summer school, summer camp, or in any other summer program, you will find that the summer months can be loaded with learning that's full of fun, too.

The book is organized by great summer topics: BUGS, because they seem to be everywhere this time of year; PATRIOTISM, because nothing could be more American than Independence Day; OLD FRIENDS, NEW FRIENDS, because children are getting ready to leave one class and enter another; and SUMMER FUN, because…well, that one is pretty obvious. The activities—many contributed by teachers from around the country—cover math, science, music, art, social studies, history, movement, language arts, and literacy, often combining a few areas in one activity. For example, "Collaborative Bug Banner" (see page 10) includes research, reading, writing, science, and art. "Friendship Hearts" (see page 26) combines math, language arts, social studies, and movement. You'll also find:

- a reproducible send-home activity calendar
- a fun and easy no-cook recipe based on a favorite story
- ready-to-use reproducible pages, including an emergent reader mini-play and Bug Bingo
- easy-to-learn songs children will love to sing again and again
- web site connections plus a computer pen pal program
- a movement activity that makes transition times fun
- literature links from old favorites to new classics
- an interactive mini-book for children to make and keep
- an interactive friendship pocket calendar
- a beautiful full-color poetry poster, featuring "two friends" by Nikki Giovanni
- and many more summertime treats!

Throughout this book, you'll find web site suggestions to support various activities. Please remember that Internet locations and contents can change over time. We cannot guarantee the availability of sites recommended in this book at the time of publication.

Multiple Intelligences Connections

Your students learn in different ways—some are more verbal, others prefer written expression. Some are comfortable working in groups, others like independent projects. Some children's strengths lie in music, art, and other modes of expression. To help you meet your students' needs and encourage all of their strengths, you'll find all these learning modalities woven into the activities in this book.

Name _____

Summer Activity Calendar

Choose _____ activities to do each week this month. Ask an adult in your family to initial the square in the box of each activity you complete. Bring this paper back to school on _____.

Monday	Tuesday	Wednesday	Thursday	Friday
Write your first and last name on a sheet of paper. Cut apart the letters. Use the letters to make new words.	Look at a calendar. Find the first day of summer. How many days until autumn?	Go on a rainbow hunt. Find something for each color of the rainbow: red, orange, yellow, green, blue, purple.	Make up a story about how the sun came to be. Share your story with someone.	People can *walk*, *skip*, and *run*. Name other words for ways people can move.
What word describes you? Ask a family member to help you look it up in a dictionary. What does this word mean?	Think of a word that describes a family member. Look it up together in a dictionary. What does it mean?	What are the dates for each Wednesday in July? The numbers make a pattern. Add four numbers to the pattern.	Pretend you're a caterpillar. Act out your life cycle! 	Talk about sun safety with a family member. Draw a picture that shows how to stay safe in the sun.
Look at this butterfly. Find a matching butterfly on this page.	Veins carry food and water through a leaf. Look at a leaf. Trace the path the food and water take.	Read a book with someone in your family. Take turns retelling the story. Include as many details as you can.	Look at a calendar. How many months until your birthday? How many weeks?	Make a musical instrument. Place sand or uncooked rice in a paper cup. Tape paper over the top. Shake it while you sing!
Fire + fly = firefly! Can you make three more words that start with fire?	Collect 20 small stones or shells. (Ask a grownup in your family to help you.) How many ways can you sort them?	Use your pebbles or shells to make number sentences. How many ways can you show the number 20?	Look at the words on this page. Can you find two that rhyme with *play*?	Turn *Summer* into a tongue twister! Make up a sentence using as many words as you can that start with s.

Bugs

Bug Match

Use Bug Bingo insect cards to play a matching game. Mix up the cards and place them facedown in rows. Let children take turns flipping two cards faceup. If the cards match, the player keeps them. If not, the cards go facedown again and it's the next player's turn.

SCIENCE

Bug Bingo

Build science vocabulary with a game of Bug Bingo. Make copies of the Bug Bingo activity sheets on pages 12 and 13. Cut out the insect cards and place them in a paper bag. Make multiple copies of the four game boards, cut them apart, and give one to each child. Give each child several Bingo markers—any small manipulative will do—from math unit cubes to dried beans. Reach into the bag and pick a card. Read the name of the bug and show the picture to children. Children with matching bugs on their game boards put a marker on the bug. Continue until someone has a line of four markers in a row: vertical, horizontal, or diagonal. The child then calls out "Bug Bingo!" and the game can begin again.

When the Fly Flew In...
by Lisa Westberg Peters (Penguin USA, 1994; Scholastic Trumpet Club Special Edition, 1996)

Children will love the wild, slapstick events and illustrations in this book about a tiny bug that seems to be making a great big mess! After sharing the story, take a "picture walk" back through the book. Look for clues that lead to the surprising ending.

SCIENCE

Insect or Not?

Explore how creepy-crawly creatures are alike and different. Start by asking children to call out names of bugs and other creepy crawlies they know. Record children's suggestions on sentence strips and cut so that each creature is on a separate piece. Make a two-column chart labeled "Insects" and "Non-Insects." Ask children what they think insects have in common. Discuss common attributes: three body parts (head, thorax, and abdomen), six legs and wings.

One at a time, hold up each sentence strip piece and read the name of the creature. Ask children if they think the creature is an insect or not. Place the sentence strips in the columns children suggest, using removable wall adhesive. Follow up by looking for pictures of each creature in books or on the web. Have children look carefully for the insect attributes: *Does it have six legs? three body parts?* Have children reorganize the chart according to what they discover. Leave the chart up for reference and exploration. Children can remove the creatures' names and try re-sorting them.

> Book Break

The Very Hungry Caterpillar
by Eric Carle (Putnam, 1994)

This classic story introduces children to many concepts, including the days of the week, numbers, and the life cycle of a butterfly. After reading the story for pure enjoyment, let children plan and prepare a snack fit for a hungry caterpillar—and hungry children! (See Caterpillar's School-Day Snack, below.) To further explore concepts introduced in the book, see A Caterpillar's Calendar, below.

SCIENCE, LANGUAGE ARTS, ART

A Caterpillar's Calendar

After sharing *The Very Hungry Caterpillar*, try this story-mapping activity to learn more.

- Make a story map by dividing a sheet of craft paper into seven sections—one for each day of the week. Let children tell you the days of the week, in order, using the book for help. Write them across the top of the story map.

- Invite a child to draw a picture to show what happened on Sunday. (*The caterpillar came out of the egg.*) Have other volunteers use words and pictures to record what the caterpillar ate from Monday to Saturday.

- Let children use this graphic organizer to retell the story to you and one another. Follow up by asking children to point out each stage in the caterpillar's life. Introduce the word *metamorphosis* and use the activity as an introduction to a lesson on life cycles.

MATH, SOCIAL STUDIES

Caterpillar's School-Day Snack

After reading *The Very Hungry Caterpillar*, ask children to tell you what the caterpillar ate on the days they go to school. Review what the caterpillar ate on these days and list the foods on chart paper: 1 apple, 2 pears, 3 plums, 4 strawberries, 5 oranges. Gather the ingredients and prepare them for children to work with (remove plum pits, peel oranges, cut away strawberry tops, core apple and pears). Give children blunt or plastic knives and let them work on paper plates or cutting boards to cut up the fruit. Have children place the fruit in a big bowl, then serve and enjoy their snack!

Check for allergies before serving.

Bugs

LANGUAGE ARTS, SCIENCE

"The Riddle of the Bugs" Mini-Play

Explore rhyming words and give children a chance to express their dramatic flair with the mini-play on page 15. Copy the play on chart paper. Read it through with children, then invite them to find rhyming pairs, such as *sting* and *thing*. Give each child a copy of the play, assign parts, and create simple costumes—for example, attach pipe cleaners to a construction-paper headband for antennae. Let children rehearse, then perform their play for an audience. Repeat the play several times so that children can play different parts.

Teacher Share

SCIENCE, MATH, LANGUAGE ARTS

Closeup on Bugs

Take a nature walk to investigate insects. Use "bug-catchers" (available at science and teacher supply stores) if you can, but regular jars with holes poked in the lids will also do. Encourage children to try to catch bugs they recognize. The best way to do this is to creep up quietly, gently place the jar on the ground, and let the bug crawl in. (Be sure to caution children to steer clear of bugs that might sting or bite, such as bees and fire ants.) When children have several insects in the jar, return to the classroom for a closer look: *What are the bugs doing?*

Make a math connection by letting children write number sentences and stories about their bugs. Children can draw the bugs, then write number sentences beneath the pictures—for example, 2 ladybugs + 3 ants = 5 bugs. (See sample, left.) Go further by having children turn their number sentences into short stories—for example, *I went on a nature walk to collect bugs and I found a ladybug. Next I found two ants. I found another ladybug and one more ant. All together, I found five bugs.* Be sure to return the insects to their natural habitats before too long.

Bobbie Williams
Brookwood Elementary School
Snellville, Georgia

If you live in an area that makes it difficult to look for insects outside, consider purchasing little plastic bugs (sold in toy and school-supply stores). Let children pick a handful without looking and place them in a jar. They can complete the activities as described using the toy bugs.

Teacher Share

MUSIC, SCIENCE

The Buggy Song

Children (and adults!) tend to learn facts better when there's a tune to go with them. To help children learn the criteria needed to classify a creature as an insect, sing this song to the tune of "The Farmer in the Dell." (Note that not all insects have antennae.)

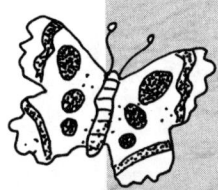

> Antennae and six legs
> Antennae and six legs
> Insects can have them both you know
> Antennae and six legs.
>
> Head, thorax, abdomen
> Head, thorax, abdomen
> An insect has three body parts
> Head, thorax, abdomen.

You can make up little teaching songs easily: The words don't need to rhyme, they just need to fit roughly into the rhythm of a familiar children's tune. How about "Old MacDonald"?

> Old MacDonald had some bugs, E-I-E-I-O.
> And one of these bugs, it was a bee, E-I-E-I-O.
> With a buzz-buzz here, and a buzz-buzz there...

That's a start...you (and the children) do the rest!

Rita Galloway
Bonham Elementary School
Harlingen, Texas

Computer Connection

Try these web sites to learn more about bugs.

gnv.ifas.ufl.edu/ ~tjw/recbk.htm
Check *The Book of Insect Records* to find out the fastest flier, fastest wing beat, loudest, heaviest, longest, and more!

www.thebugpage .com/orders/
Click on the name of the insect you want to learn about.

dir.yahoo.com/ Science/Biology/ Zoology/Animals _Insects_and_ Pets/
Click on "Insects" for more than 500 links to related sites.

Bugs

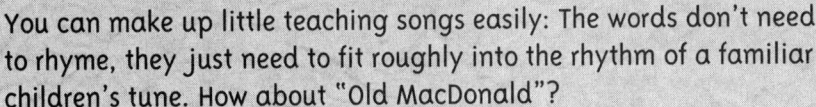

Audubon First Field Guides: Insects
(Scholastic, 1999)

Easy-to-read text and more than 450 photographs help students get to know the insects around them. A removable, water-resistant "spotter's guide" makes it easy to identify insects anywhere.

Bugs

> SCIENCE, LANGUAGE ARTS, ART

Collaborative Bug Banner

Make copies of the bug banner activity sheet on page 14 and give one to each child. Ask children to choose a bug they'd like to learn more about. Some suggestions might be ladybugs, butterflies, beetles, dragonflies, grasshoppers, bees, and so on. Have children write the name of their bug on the sheet, then conduct research to learn more—for example, *What does the bug eat? What is something special it can do?* (See Book Break, below, for suggested resources.) Have children use words and pictures to record information.

To create the banner, cut out a simple circle shape for a head, and draw a smiling face. Tape two pipe cleaners to the top, and attach the head to the wall. As children complete their bug banner pages, have them cut out the shapes along the dashed line, and tape them one after another to the bug's head. Soon you will have a beautiful bug banner crawling around your classroom!

> Book Break

A Bug Research Library
(What Is an Insect?, What Do Insects Do?, Where Do Insects Live?, Bugs, Bugs, Bugs!, Spider Names)
Insects and Spiders Emergent Readers (Scholastic, 1998)

These 12-page books, with colorful photos and simple text, are perfect for independent research. Teachers' notes in the back of each book provide additional information.

Teacher Share

MATH

Ladybug Math Story Mat

Make copies of the math story mat on page 16. Give children red crayons or markers, and let them color in their ladybugs without adding spots. Make a set of small black construction-paper circles, about ten for each child. Share math stories that students can act out with the black spots on their story mats. Look at different ways children solve the problems. Samples follow.

- **For addition:** The first ladybug had three dots. The second ladybug had four. How many did they have all together?

- **For subtraction:** The first ladybug had five dots. The second ladybug had three, but then she lost one. How many do they have all together?

- **For logical thinking:** The two ladybugs had nine dots all together. The ladybug on the right had fewer than the ladybug on the left. How many dots could each ladybug have?

Bob Krech
Dutch Neck School
Princeton Junction, New Jersey

SCIENCE, MATH, SNACK

One Honey of a Treat!

Talk about bees with children. A lot of people don't like bees because they can sting. But bees can also do a wonderful thing—make honey! Older honeybees suck *nectar*, a sweet liquid, out of flowers. They feed the nectar to younger bees. The bees have a "honey machine" right inside their stomachs! It's called a *honey sac*. Inside the honey sac, the nectar gets thicker and turns into honey. When it's ready, the honey comes out the bee's mouth and is stored in the hive. Celebrate bees with this delicious and nutritious treat.

- Measure 4 cups of milk and pour into a blender or bowl. Add 4 scoops frozen yogurt and 3 tablespoons honey.

- If blending by hand, let children take turns stirring the mixture with a wire whisk. If using a blender, blend on high speed until the mixture is frothy. Pour the mixture into small drinking cups. Enjoy the honey milkshake, and don't forget to thank the bees!

TIP

Before serving, check for milk or honey allergies.

Bug Bingo Cards

Activity Page

 Praying Mantis	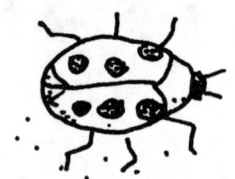 Ladybug	 Beetle
 Butterfly	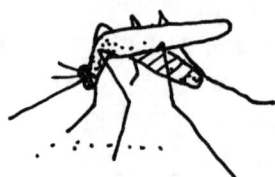 Mosquito	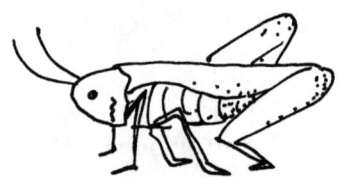 Grasshopper
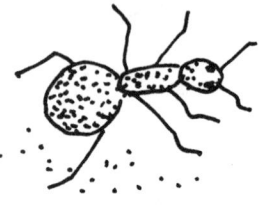 Ant	 Bee	 Fly
 Dragonfly	 Moth	 Wasp
 Katydid	 Cicada	 Cricket
 Locust	 Treehopper	 Water Strider

Fresh & Fun Summer Scholastic Professional Books

Bug Bingo Boards

Activity Page

Bug Bingo

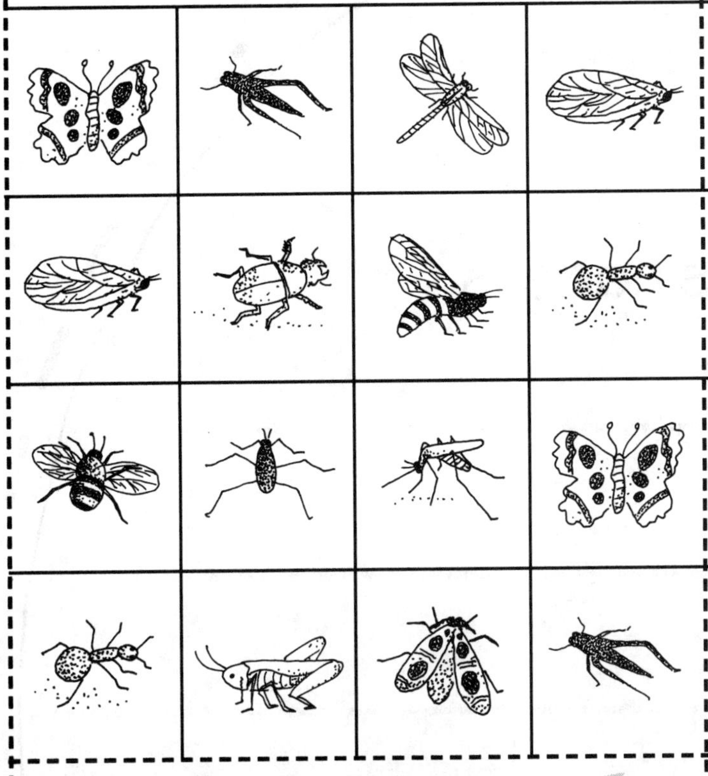

Bug Bingo

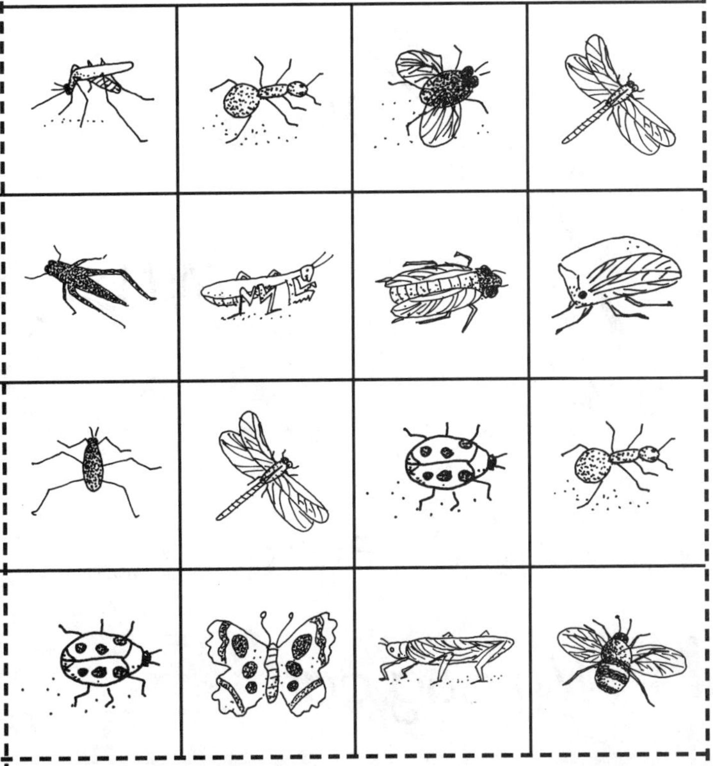

Bug Bingo

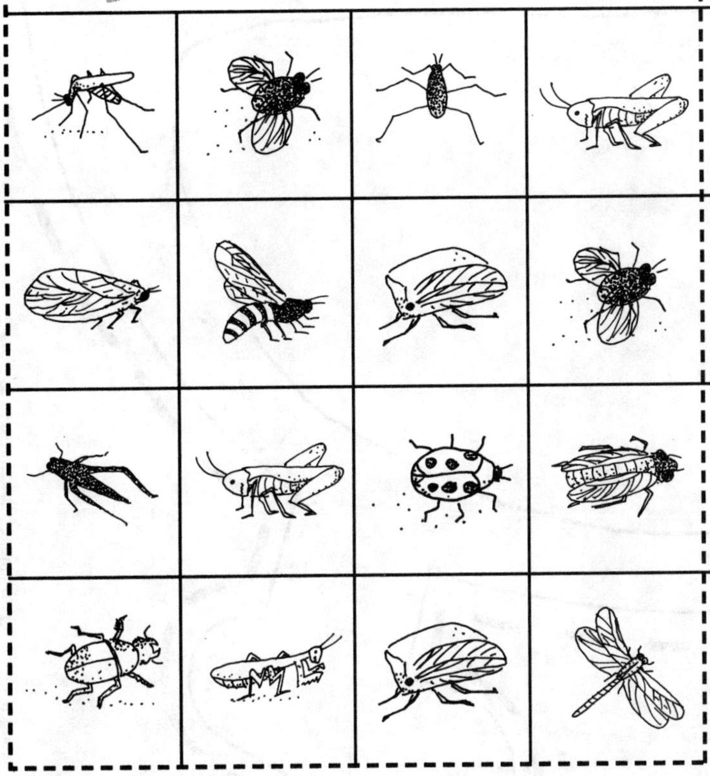

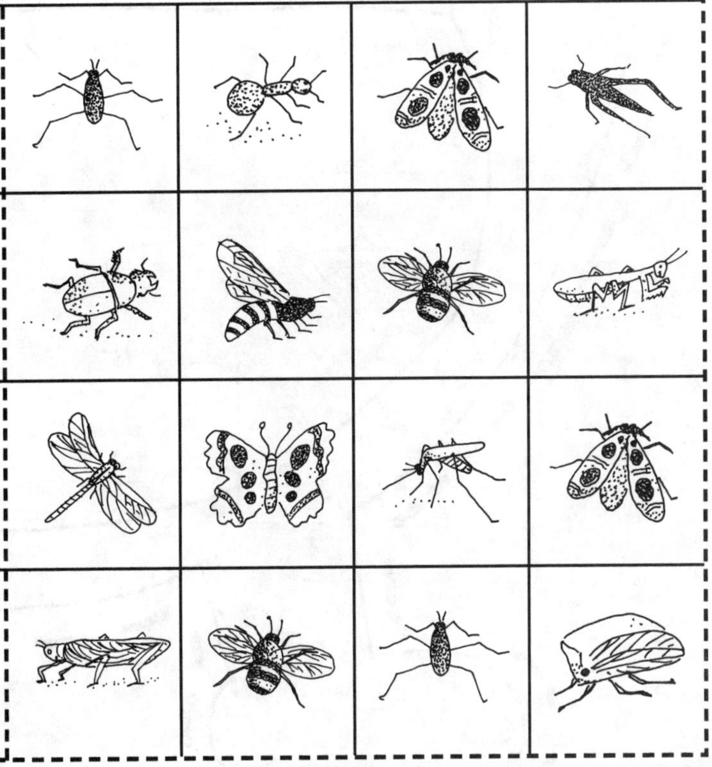

Bug Bingo

13

Activity Page

Collaborative Bug Banner

Name _____

My bug's name is

_____

My bug eats _____

My bug can _____

My bug looks like this:

Fresh & Fun Summer   Scholastic Professional Books

Activity Page

The Riddle of the Bugs
by Pamela Chanko

Characters
(to be played by small groups of students)

Children ❁ Bees ❁ Mosquitoes ❁ Caterpillars/Butterflies ❁ Ladybugs

Children: Where did all
These bugs come from?
Listen to them
Buzz and hum.

Bees: We are bugs,
We can sting.
But we make honey,
A yummy thing!

Mosquitoes: We are bugs,
We sting, too.
Better watch out.
We might sting you!

Children: Where did all
These bugs come from?
Listen to them
Buzz and hum.

All Bugs: Summer is here!
Summer is here!
We all come out
This time of year.

**Caterpillars/
Butterflies:** We are bugs,
We don't sting.
We crawl now
But we'll grow wings.

Ladybugs: We are bugs,
Red with spots.
The spots are small,
But we've got lots!

Children: Bugs are playing
Little games.
They want us
To guess their names.

Bees make honey.
Mosquitoes sting.
Ladybugs have spots.
Caterpillars grow wings.

All Bugs: They guessed
our secret names,
Oh no!
No time for games.
It's time to go!

Fresh & Fun Summer Scholastic Professional Books

15

Activity Page

Name _____

Date _____

Ladybug Math Story Mat

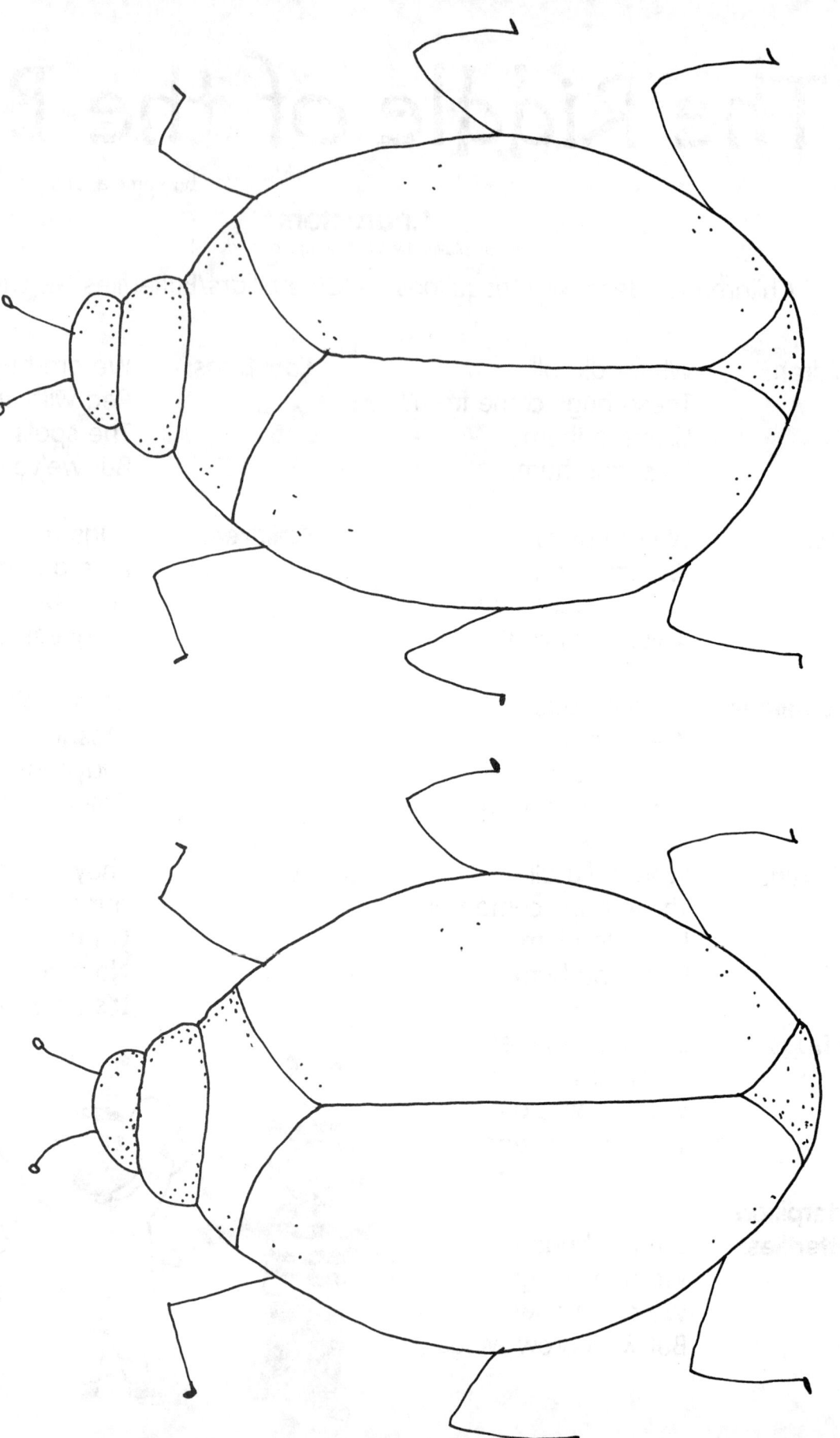

Teacher Share

ART, SOCIAL STUDIES

Independence Day Parade

Children will have fun making mini "floats" for an Independence Day Parade. Give each child a shoebox (lids not needed) to decorate with paint, markers, crayons, feathers, stickers, glitter, and, of course, anything red, white, or blue! Have children bring a stuffed animal or doll to school on parade day and place it on the float. String the boxes together by stapling one to the next with pieces of yarn. On the day of the parade, play a march (Sousa marches always work well) and have children march through the halls, leading their floats to the beat of the music and a cheering audience!

Mary Jane Banta
Northeastern Elementary School
Fountain City, Indiana

SOCIAL STUDIES

Secret Ballot Box

Explore the concept of voting—one of the ways Americans participate in the political process—by setting up a class ballot box.

- Introduce the activity by asking children what they know about voting. Explain that this is how the president and other people in our government get their jobs.

- Make a class ballot box to give children an opportunity to vote on class decisions. Have children decorate a shoebox top and bottom with a patriotic theme. Cut a slit in the top and place it on the box bottom.

- Give each child a copy of the secret ballot slips on page 20. Have children cut apart the ballots and complete the first one to vote on a class snack. (Depending on the size of your class, you may wish to write two or three choices—such as crackers, pretzels, and fruit—on the chalkboard.)

- When everyone has placed their ballots in the box, remove the lid and take a count.

- Use the other ballots as you choose: every few days, once a week, and so on. Make new ballots to take votes on other class decisions, such as when to have free-choice time.

Patriotism

TIP

For a variation on the Independence Day Parade, plan an Appreciation Parade to celebrate America. Initiate a discussion about what is special about our country's people and places. Have children create flags to carry in a parade, using words and pictures to tell something they appreciate about their country. They can use sturdy paper for the flags, then attach them to yardstick-length dowels.

Patriotism

Book Break

Betsy Ross
by Alexandra Wallner (Holiday House, 1998)

Set in Colonial Philadelphia, this charming book tells the story of Betsy Ross's life, including her most famous accomplishment—the sewing of the first American flag. Children will love the details of eighteenth-century American life and the descriptions of Revolutionary times. After reading, let children follow Betsy's directions in the back of the book as she teaches them how to make a five-pointed star in just one snip!

Computer Connection

For facts about the Statue of Liberty, including measurements, go to

www.nps.gov/stli/

SOCIAL STUDIES, MATH

Measure the Statue of Liberty

Almost all children have seen pictures of the Statue of Liberty, but not many have seen it up close. This measuring activity will help children understand just how big this national symbol is.

- On green paper, draw the outline of an eye measuring 2 feet, 6 inches across. (You may need to tape two sheets of paper together.) Do the same for the lips: The correct measurement is 3 feet across. Set these aside.

- Give children non-standard units of measurement. (Unifix cubes work well because they can be counted by tens.) Show children a photograph of the statue and point to one of the eyes. Ask: *On the real statue, how many units would it take to get across the eye?* Have children record estimates. Do the same for the mouth.

- Display the actual-size drawing of the eye and mouth. Let children revise their estimates, then measure! *If just one eye is that large, how big do they think the whole statue is?*

Mitzi Fehl
Poquoson Primary School
Poquoson, Virginia

ART, SOCIAL STUDIES

Design a Class Flag

What does America's flag stand for? Invite children to share their thoughts, then read *The Flag We Love* to learn more. (See Book Break, below.) Investigate other countries' flags (see Computer Connection, right), then work together to create a class flag. Discuss what the class flag will stand for, then brainstorm colors, designs, symbols, and so on. Make a sketch, then create the flag. Hang your class flag proudly outside your door. Children may want to salute it each day as they come in!

Book Break

The Flag We Love
by Pamela Munoz Ryan (Charlesbridge Publishing, 1996)

Each right-facing page of this inventive book is a colorful painting of the American flag under different circumstances: being raised in front of a log schoolhouse, at the Vietnam memorial, even on the moon! Each left-facing page includes a smaller picture, and facts about the flag and the event.

MUSIC, SOCIAL STUDIES

Singing and Signing the Red, White, and Blue

Part of being a patriotic American lies in appreciating the diversity of our nation. This includes showing respect and consideration for people who speak different languages and have special needs. You can touch on these concepts while teaching about the American flag with this song.

(Sing to the tune of "Three Blind Mice.")

Red, white, blue,
Red, white, blue,
I love you,
I love you.

Oh what a wonderful sight to see,
A flag for you and a flag for me,
It means we live in a land that's free,
Red, white, blue.

Write the words to the song on chart paper, and sing it a few times with children. Once children are familiar with the song, teach them the hand signs that go along with it. (See illustrations, below.)

love you   red   white   blue

Patriotism

Computer Connection

Learn more about the American flag with these web sites.

w3f.com/gifs/flag/country/index.html
View pictures of nearly 200 flags, representing countries from Afghanistan to Zimbabwe.

www.ushistory.org/betsy/index.html
Flag facts, history, trivia, even theories about what the colors stand for.

To learn more about ASL, check out the following web sites. Some even provide animation!

www.bconnex.net/~randys/index_nf.html

where.com/scott.net/asl/

commtechlab.msu.edu/sites/aslweb/

Secret Ballot Box

 Activity Page

Secret Ballot

I think
we should have

―――――――――

for snack.

Secret Ballot

I think
we should read

―――――――――

at story time.

Secret Ballot

I think
we should do

―――――――――

for our group project.

Secret Ballot

I think our class
show-and-tell theme
should be

――――――――― .

Old Friends, New Friends

LANGUAGE ARTS, ART

Teaching With the Poster "two friends"

Display the poetry poster in your classroom as you explore the concept of friendship. Use the lessons that follow for a month of poetry among pals!

Week 1: Draw a Poem
Read the poem aloud before displaying it. Tell children you will continue rereading the poem and that you would like them to draw what they hear. Read slowly and repeat as many times as needed. When children are finished, let them turn around and compare their interpretations with the poster. What are the similarities and differences?

Week 2: Number Sentence Poems
Use "two friends" to reinforce number concepts. Read it to children, pointing out its use of numbers. Then have children pair up to think of four to eight things about themselves that can be made into number sentences. For example: William and Alicia are working together. William has two shirts on. Alicia has only one. 2 + 1 = 3 shirts.

Week 3: Friendship Possibilities
In the poem "two friends," the writer describes the similarities and differences between two good friends. Gather children in an open area. Put children's names in a paper bag and select two at a time in random order. The two chosen students stand up in front of the group. Ask the group (including the standing pair) to suggest similarities and differences that might make these children good friends. Do they both play similar games outdoors? Do they like different foods they might trade at lunchtime? If children need help getting started, make a few observations you feel are relevant and ask if they agree.

Week 4: The Book of Friendships
As a culminating tribute to friendship, have children write poems about a friend of their own. Children might start their poems as Nikki Giovanni began "two friends": "lydia and shirley have…" (using their own names, of course), then list the things that make them friends. Have children illustrate their poems and bind them to make a class book. It is guaranteed to be one children will return to again and again!

Old Friends, New Friends

Book Break

Best Friends for Frances
by Russell Hoban (HarperCollins, 1976)

This classic story has all the "Frances" trademark elements: funny, repetitive, childlike dialogue; seemingly endless food lists; a conflict resolved in an interesting way; and, of course, plenty of offbeat ditties sung by Frances. In this one, Frances ignores her little sister in order to gain the attention of her "best friend" Albert. For a fun follow-up, why not make up a Frances-style "song" together? Remember—the last few lines don't always have to rhyme. Frances likes her freedom!

Language Arts, Social Studies, Technology

Twenty-First Century Pen Pals

A great way to make new friends is to get a pen pal. And the most modern way to do this is, of course, on the Internet! Set up an e-mail pen pal program for your class. These programs can be a wonderful way to make new friends, learn about different cultures, and get children writing! There are plenty of web sites to help you get started. Suggestions follow.

- **www.ks-connection.org/** Pen Pal Box is a wonderful site designed especially for children. It features pen pals sorted by classrooms and age groups.

- **www.ozkidz.gil.com.au/rm/student/surfe.html** Surf-E-Mates includes a link to the Kid City Post Office, as well as a link called "Class Projects: Intercultural E-Mail Classroom Connections," specifically designed to coordinate e-mail projects with classrooms around the world.

- **www.worldwide.edu/planning_guide/Pen_Pals/PenPals.html** World Wide Classroom Pen Pals provides a host of links to pen pal program resources around the world.

Book Break

Best Friends
by Steven Kellogg (Penguin Putnam, 1986)

Kathy and Louise are best friends, but that doesn't mean they always get along. After sharing the story, let children talk about times they've experienced difficulties, such as jealousy, in their friendships. What did they do about it? Depending on the age level of your students, you might want to have a group discussion or use the question as a writing prompt.

MATH, SOCIAL STUDIES

Friendship Pocket Calendar

This class calendar will encourage acts of friendship every day!

- Write the month and year across the top of a sheet of tagboard. Underneath, write the days of the week left to right, Sunday through Saturday. Write numbers (1–31) on the outside of empty library card pockets for the dates. (Check school-supply stores and catalogs.)

- Glue the pockets to the tagboard in numerical order, starting with the first day of the month. Display the calendar.

- Give each child an index card. Discuss things people do to show love and caring for friends—for example, with a hug, by doing someone a favor, by giving someone a compliment, and so on. Have children write an "act of friendship" on one side of their index card. (To fill out the calendar, you may want to add a few cards of your own, or have some children write two cards.)

- Place the cards in the pockets with the blank side facing out. Each morning, turn over the card in that day's pocket. It is each child's "mission" to accomplish the act of friendship written on the card at least once by the end of the day.

Old Friends, New Friends

TIP

You might want to write the "friendship mission" of the day on the chalkboard and have children write their initials next to it once they have accomplished it. At the end of each day, children can describe the situation and what they did.

Teacher Share

LANGUAGE ARTS, SOCIAL STUDIES

Secret Pal Messages

This "secret pal" activity is a great way for children to make new friends. On a Monday, put children's names in a paper bag and have each child pick one. The name they picked will be the person they will write secret messages to. Talk with children about writing positive messages and let them suggest some—for example, "I like you because…you are a good friend." Have children write and deliver (to classroom mailboxes and cubbies) their secret messages (no names!) each day from Monday through Thursday. On Friday, have children write their last message, signing it with their first initial only. Allow extra time for children to guess their secret pals.

Bobbie Williams
Brookwood Elementary School
Snellville, Georgia

I am glad I picked your name. I like you! From, your secret friend

Old Friends, New Friends

TIP

If children have trouble getting pictures from home, and have old and new friends at the same school, you might want to bring in an instant or digital camera one day and help them take photos themselves! If photos are unavailable, children can always draw pictures of their friends.

LANGUAGE ARTS

Old Friends and New Friends Mini-Book

In advance, ask parents and children to find photos of one old friend and one new friend to bring in from home. Give each child a copy of page 27. Have children cut along the dotted lines and tape A to B. Guide children in completing each page to tell about their old friends. Have children flip the paper and tell a story about a new friend, using the "old friend" sentences as a model. (Have them substitute the word *new* for *old*.) When children are finished, they can add illustrations, and fold their pages back and forth to make accordian books.

Teacher Share

SOCIAL STUDIES

Facts About Friends

Use this giant Venn diagram to let children explore the many ways they can be friends.

- Have children write several facts about themselves on index cards, one fact per card. Encourage children to stick to such things as likes and dislikes, favorite hobbies, and so on, rather than facts such as "I have red hair" or "I'm wearing a green shirt." Have children write their names on an index card, too.

- Gather children in an open area and overlap two hula-hoops on the floor. Invite two children to try the activity. Have them place their name cards above the circles. Then let them take turns sharing their fact cards aloud. If both children "share the fact" it goes in the overlapping section. Otherwise, children put their cards in their individual circles.

Rita Galloway
Bonham Elementary School
Harlingen, Texas

TIP

This can be done with endless combinations of children; once they understand how it works, it can easily become a center activity children can do on their own.

Old Friends, New Friends

> MUSIC

Silver and Gold Friendship Circles

This is a great activity for transition times, such as finding partners or preparing to go home. Practice the following traditional song with children:

> Make new friends and keep the old,
> One is silver and the other gold.

Once children are familiar with the song, divide the group in half and have them form two circles by holding hands. One circle should be inside the other, so that children in the inside circle are facing those in the outside circle. Have them sing the song as the circles move in opposite directions. When children reach the word "gold," they must stop moving. Whomever they are facing is their partner! If using the activity to prepare for going home, keep repeating the song after each pair goes to their cubbies. This is both a lovely way to end the day and a great way to avoid the cubby crush!

> SOCIAL STUDIES

Old Friends...Young Friends!

One nice aspect of intergenerational friendships is the capacity they have to teach. Older people can teach younger people things they have learned from experience. Younger people can teach older people new ways of looking at the world. Have children write and/or dictate a story about something they have learned from an older friend—for example, a special way to make cookies, something about their friend's hometown, or even how to take care of a pet parakeet. Repeat the activity for something they have taught their older friends. Have children illustrate their pages and bind them together to create a class book about these special friendships.

Book Break

Wilfrid Gordon McDonald Partridge
by Mem Fox (Kane/Miller, 1991)

"There was once a small boy named Wilfrid Gordon McDonald Partridge and what's more he wasn't very old either. His house was next door to an old people's home and he knew all the people who lived there." Miss Nancy is Wilfrid's favorite. But one day Wilfrid overhears his parents saying that Miss Nancy has lost her memory. Wilfrid asks all his friends at the home what a *memory* is...something warm, something as precious as gold, something that makes you laugh. Wilfrid collects his interpretations of these things, and gives them to Miss Nancy one by one. And bit by bit, she begins to remember.

Old Friends, New Friends

Book Break

Free To Be...You and Me
conceived by Marlo Thomas (McGraw Hill, 1974)

This collection of poems, songs, and stories encourages friendship by fostering children's own self-confidence, thereby encouraging them to reach out to others, be empathetic, and respect people's feelings. NOTE: If you have trouble finding the original printing listed above, try *Free To Be...You and Me and Free to be a Family*, created by Marlo Thomas (Running Press, 1997). This updated version includes the original material with some new additions.

MATH, LANGUAGE ARTS

Friendship Hearts

This activity can strengthen a range of skills and will get children together who may not ordinarily spend time with one another.

- Make sets of matching hearts to pair up children in your class. Your matches can reflect any skill you'd like to reinforce. For example, you can strengthen addition skills by writing number sentences with the same sum on matching hearts. Or make matches to practice word families—for example, write words that contain the same phonogram on matching cards (*pack, quack; dog, frog*).

- Use removable wall adhesive to stick the hearts in children's cubbies. You may do this randomly, or you may want to take this opportunity to pair up children who don't often spend time together.

- When children come to school the next morning, have them stick their hearts to the fronts of their shirts or sweaters. Then have them find their matching heart! Explain that children with matching hearts are "Fast Friends"— they will do special things together that day. (You can plan a special activity or project in advance, have partners sit with each other for lunch or snack, make a simple gift, and so on.) At the end of the day, gather children together to exchange their gifts and talk about the experience.

Catherine Wenglowski
Beginnings School
New York, New York

Activity Page

My Old Friend

by ....

1

Put a picture of your friend here.

A

I have an old friend named ....

2

B

I like ....
because ....
....

3

We like to ....
....
....

4

Summer Fun

TIP

There are a lot of subjects you can cover using a beach ball and this general format. You can make it a language arts activity by putting story starters on the ball and having students continue the story as it gets tossed. You can add a new twist to discussions by having each child who catches the ball name a favorite thing to do in the summertime. The possibilities are many...why not make up a game of your own?

Teacher Share

MATH

Beach Ball Math

This activity is fabulous for adding summer fun to math practice, and it couldn't be easier! Pick up an ordinary beach ball, the kind with different-colored stripes. On each color (or every other), place a strip of masking tape with a different number sentence on it (2 + 3, 7 – 4, 3 x 2...the level of difficulty depends on the age group you are working with). Indoors or out, gather children in a circle. Toss the ball to one of them. Ask this child to choose the color under one of his or her hands, then read the number sentence on that color, give the answer, and toss it back to you. Continue, tossing the ball to a different child each time until everyone has had a turn. As children become familiar with the number sentences, you can try to make the game go faster and faster! Then you can change the math problems on the ball and start over.

Deborah Rovin-Murphy
Richboro Elementary School
Richboro, Pennsylvania

MATH, SCIENCE

Hide-and-Seek With Shells

This game is sure to delight children of any age group. Follow these steps to play.

- Fill your sand and water table with sand. (You can also use a sandbox or large plastic tub.)
- Give each child a large-size crayon, a plain piece of paper, and a shell. (Try to make the shells as different as possible.) Have children make shell rubbings. Collect the rubbings and post them on a bulletin board near the sand table.
- Now the mystery begins! Collect all the shells and have children turn their backs as you hide them in the sand. Then let children turn around and start digging! The object of the game is to find shells and match them to rubbings. Remind children that careful observation, not speed, is the key.

Summer Fun

Book Break

Greetings From Sandy Beach
by Bob Graham (Kane/Miller, 1992)

This humorous book reads like one long, funny postcard from a good friend. When a family arrives at their designated campsite, the vacation seems doomed: They find a gang of bikers and Dad warns, "Don't go near them." However, the story shows that appearances can be misleading, as the bikers help set up their tent and hand out ice pops. The cast of unusual but innocent, funny characters are fresh and fun, as are the illustrations.

SCIENCE, MATH, HISTORY

Sun Shadow Clock

Explain to children that long ago, the sun had a very important job: It was the only way people were able to tell time! They used the shadows the sun made on a device called a *sundial* to keep track of time. Then try this experiment to let children see how sundials work.

- Fill an empty coffee can with wet sand. Stick a ruler in the middle of the sand.

- Find a sunny spot on blacktop or a sidewalk where you can draw with chalk. Make sure the spot is in open sunlight so that other shadows don't interfere.

- Place the can on the sidewalk and look for the line of the ruler's shadow. Trace over the line with chalk.

- Go out again in an hour or two and find the ruler's shadow. Again, trace the line with chalk. Continue checking and tracing every hour or two throughout the day. *In what direction are the lines moving? How far apart are they?* Compare the lines to those on the clock in your classroom. You just might see a similarity!

Remind children not to look directly at the sun.

Book Break

Sun Song
by Jean Marzollo (HarperCollins, 1995)

The beautiful, lilting verse and glorious painted illustrations in this book follow the sun as it touches animals, people, and nature throughout the day. As each page is turned, the reader gets an intimate glimpse of a new world and how the sun is a part of it. After reading, you might ask children how the sun touches their days. Children might like to draw pictures to illustrate their responses.

Summer Fun

TIP

For a simpler (though not quite as dramatic) version of this activity, have children collect collage materials and/or natural objects and place them on dark-colored construction paper. (Stick lightweight objects to the paper with removable wall adhesive.) Set the collages in direct sunlight and move them as needed so that they stay directly in the sun. Do this for a period of a few days (be sure to pull them indoors quickly if it rains) until the color of the construction paper has faded quite a bit. (You can tell by comparing it to a new piece.) Remove the objects and see the print!

Teacher Share

ART, SCIENCE

Sun Prints

Making sun prints is both a technological and natural activity that results in spectacular outcomes. Materials for sun prints are available from several educational companies at surprisingly low prices. Using these kits is simple, and involves no chemicals. Children simply select collage items (lace, leaves, flowers, feathers, thin branches, paper cutouts, and so on) they'd like to print. Then they place them on the sun-sensitive paper and set it out in the sun for a short time. The paper develops in plain water in just a few minutes and produces a beautiful blue and white image! Following are two resources for sun print supplies.

- EDUCATIONAL INSIGHTS: **www.ierc.com/** (800) 933-3277.
- THE LAWRENCE HALL OF SCIENCE: **www.lhs.berkeley.edu/store** (510) 642-1016.

Catherine Wenglowski
Beginnings School
New York, New York

Book Break

The Way to Start a Day
by Byrd Baylor (Simon & Schuster, 1986)

In this Caldecott Honor book, Byrd Baylor describes the way to start the day in many places all over the world and throughout history: by greeting the rising sun with special words, gifts, and rituals. After reading, ask children how they like to greet the new day. Ask: *What is the first thing you do when you get up in the morning?* Together, decide on a ritual to greet each new day in the classroom. It can be very simple, such as looking out the window, finding the sun, and waving "hello" to it.

Teacher Share

ART, SCIENCE

Sun Safety Puppets

Make copies of the sun safety puppet activity sheet on page 32. Have children cut out the puppet and color it in, then glue on yarn to make hair. Ask children to draw a favorite bathing suit (or make one out of construction paper and glue it on), then glue the back of the puppet to a craft stick.

Tell children that their puppets are taking an imaginary trip to the beach. Ask: *What do they need to do before they go?* (Have them look at the remaining pictures on the activity sheet for clues.) Talk about how sunblock, sunglasses, and a shirt can help keep them safe in the sun. Have children cut out the other three items and color them in. They can use removable wall adhesive to put the sunglasses and shirt on their puppets, then place the sunblock in its hand.

Deborah Rovin-Murphy
Richboro Elementary School
Richboro, Pennsylvania

Summer Fun

Computer Connection

For sun safety facts, games, and more, try this fun-filled web page:
www.coppertone.com

TIP

Encourage children to take their puppets and props home and share a sun safety lesson with their families.

SCIENCE, MATH

Where Do Puddles Go?

Children are drawn to puddles—and are naturally curious about where they go. Introduce the water cycle with this activity.

- Find or make a puddle in a sunny spot outdoors. Find or make a puddle of approximately the same size in a shady spot. Ask children what happens to puddles after a rain shower. Record ideas on chart paper.

- Take different colors of yarn and scissors outside to measure the puddles. String the yarn around the perimeter of each puddle and snip it off where it completes the circle. Use a different color for each puddle.

- Use the yarn lengths to measure the puddles each day. Keep snipping the yarn as the puddles grow smaller. Compare the two colors of yarn each time: *Which puddle is growing smaller faster?* Keep the experiment going until one or both of the puddles is entirely gone.

- Discuss children's observations and record new ideas about what happens to puddles. Children may now recognize that the warmth and light of the sun helps to dry up water.

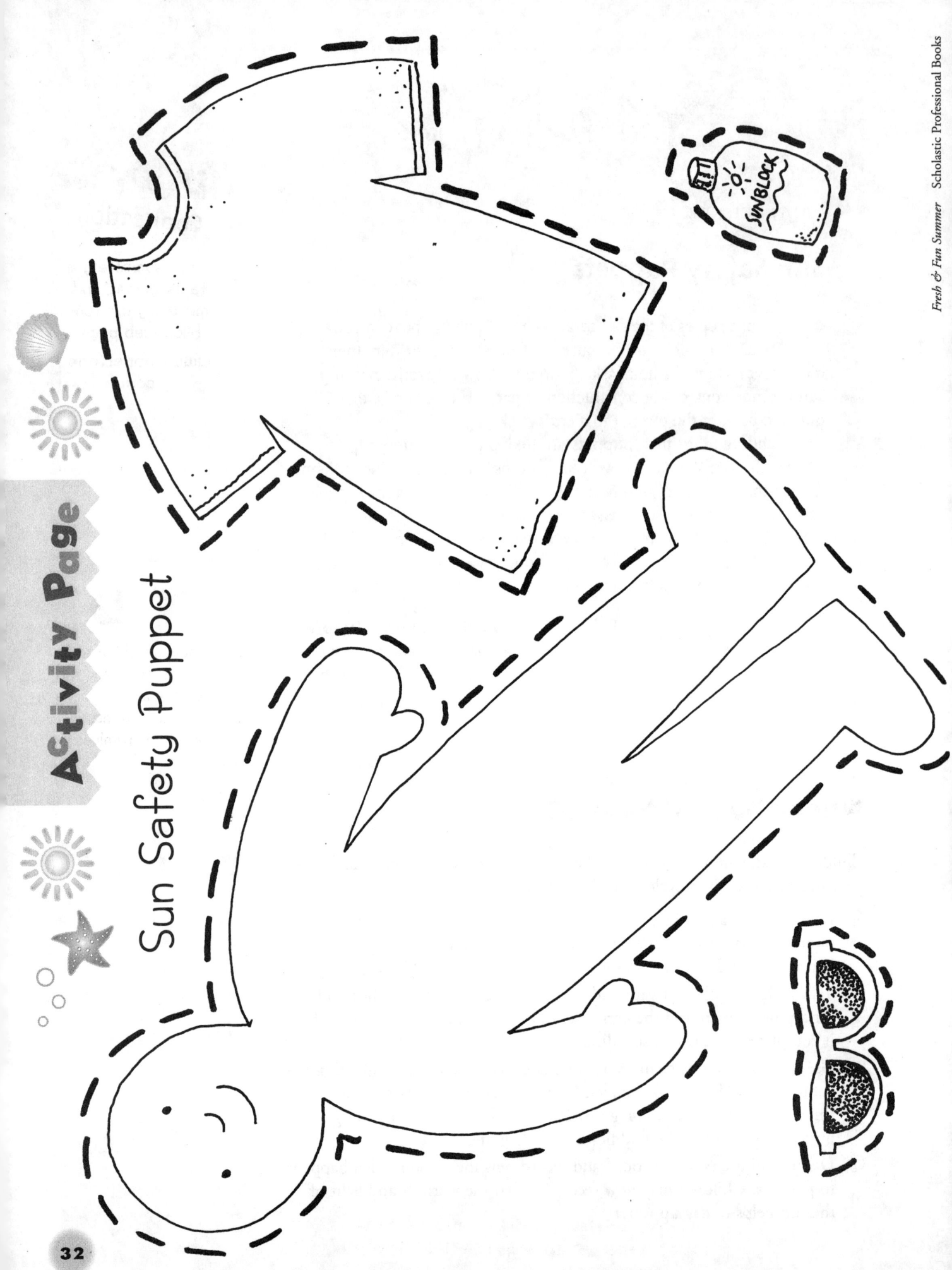

Activity Page

Sun Safety Puppet